P9-AGC-516

TWISTED WHISKERS™
I ONLY HAVE EYES FOR YOU!

Twisted Whiskers™
I Only Have Eyes
For You!

RUNNING PRESS
PHILADELPHIA • LONDON

Library of Congress Control Number: 2007929220

ISBN 978-0-7624-3175-5

This book may be ordered by mail from the publisher.
Please include $1.00 for postage and handling.
But try your bookstore first!

Running Press Book Publishers
2300 Chestnut Street
Philadelphia, PA 19103-4371

Visit us on the web!
www.runningpress.com
www.twistedwhiskers.com

INTRODUCTION

Ahh, love. That sometimes pulse-quickening, oftentimes heart-breaking, and always elusive emotion that can drive us crazy, but ultimately we can't live without. Love is what gets us through all the rainy days, the bad news, and the ups and downs (but mostly the downs) of our complicated, heart-wrenching lives. But sometimes Cupid knows us better than we know ourselves, and his arrows can induce the crazy love-struck behavior for which we more than likely have been guilty: public make-out sessions, scandalous dancing, and unrestricted hand-holding on crowded sidewalks.

There is nothing so charming as a romantic candlelit dinner or a long walk on the beach with your sweetheart. In life, all you need is love!

And what better way is there to show someone you love them than with the Twisted Whiskers™ characters? In this outrageously fun little volume, the strangely loveable creatures share some of their simple, sassy sentiments on the subject that are sure to give your special someone warm fuzzies until next Valentine's Day. If a picture is worth a thousand words, we guarantee that the irresistible images of these adorable furry friends will be worth a thousand kisses!

Did I just hear
the "L" word?

Two of a kind.

You give me
happy feet!

Wanna get frisky?

I'm a lover,
not a fighter.

16

Got anything that
needs licking?

Mmm . . .
looking tasty!

20

I'll climb to the
top for you.

Now that's HOT.

I ruff you!

Look me in the eye and
tell me I'm not cute.

I'll always be
here for you.

Fur real.

You're so
intoxicating.

Beggin' for love.

I caught the best
fish in the sea.

Who says you shouldn't date outside your species?

You give me that warm,
fuzzy feeling.

A face only
you could love.

I've seen you naked.

I'm hoppin' we stay
together forever.

48

Animal Magnetism.

Let's get our groove on.

Hey there, baby. Wanna see my hairball collection?

So in love.

Gimme some skin.

This ain't no
puppy love.

Would this
face lie to you?

"Odd couples"
are the happiest.

Love is blind.

You are the wind
beneath my wings.

Smell ya later!

Head over paws.

Serious eye candy!

I've been eyeing
you for a while.

Some tongue?

You are stunning.

I hang on every
word you say.

Mate for life.

I'm a prince inside.

You blow my mind.

I don't kiss and tell.

I'm nuts about you!

Would you be my
stinking valentine?

Love hurts.

I know it's a little corny
but...you're dam cute!

You should see
my other tricks.

Let's get wild.

Only the royal
treatment for you.

You're making
me blush!

Forgive me?

And they called
it puppy love.

You make
my heart stop.

You bring sunshine
to my life.

You are devilishly sexy.

We go
together perfectly.

This book has been bound
using handcraft methods and
Smyth-sewn to ensure durability.

The dust jacket and interior were
designed by Matt Goodman.

The text was
edited by Jennifer Leczkowski.

The text was set in
Spunky Jes and
Barnyard Gothic.